KU-362-424

All the animals shown here are in danger of becoming extinct. These species need to be saved. The giant panda is one of them.

The giant panda

Giant pandas are very easy to recognize. They are large, fluffy bears with black and white hair. Their legs, shoulders, ears, and eye patches are black.

A giant panda has ovals of black hair around its eyes.

6

Contents

Some words are shown in bold, **like this**. You can find out what they mean by looking in the Glossary.

Animals in trouble

There are many different kinds, or **species**, of animal. Some species are in danger of becoming **extinct**. This means that all the animals from that species might die.

Pandas use their sharp claws to help them climb trees.

Giant pandas mainly stay on the ground and walk on their four legs. They may climb trees to sleep or to look around. They grip things with their claws.

Where can you find giant pandas?

In the past, giant pandas lived all over southern and eastern China. They also lived in Myanmar and Vietnam. Today they only live in a few parts of South-west China.

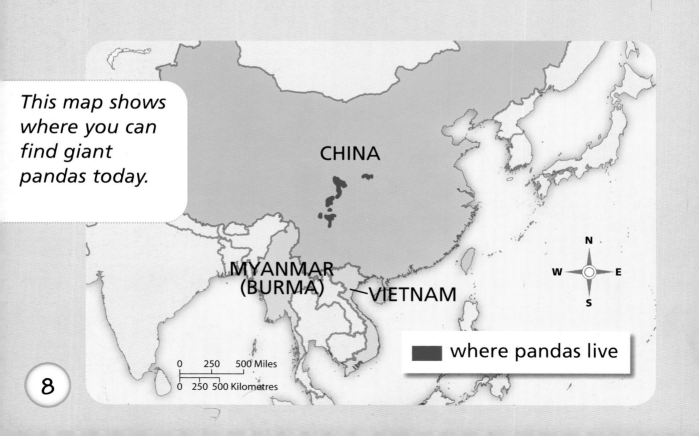

This map shows where you can find giant pandas today.

CHINA

MYANMAR
(BURMA)

VIETNAM

N
W   E
S

0   250   500 Miles
0   250 500 Kilometres

■ where pandas live

Giant pandas live on mountain slopes like these.

Giant pandas live in forests on high mountain slopes. It is cold and rainy there. The giant panda's thick, woolly hair keeps it warm and dry.

What do giant pandas eat?

Giant pandas only eat **bamboo**.
Bamboo is a kind of giant grass plant.
They eat the **shoots**, stems, and leaves
of bamboo plants.

The giant panda has
five short fingers and
a long wrist-bone.

Giant pandas have to eat a lot of bamboo to stay healthy. They can spend about 16 hours of every day eating.

Giant pandas usually sit down to eat. They hold food in their front paws.

Young giant pandas

Baby pandas are called **cubs**. They are usually born in a cave. They stay there for six weeks. Pandas are **mammals**, so the cubs drink milk from their mother.

This panda cub is about four weeks old.

Panda cubs start following their mother when they are three months old.

A cub starts to eat **bamboo** when it is four months old. It stays with its mother for two years. After that, the panda will live alone.

13

Natural dangers

Adult giant pandas are not in danger from other animals. They are too big and strong to be attacked. Snow leopards sometimes catch panda **cubs**.

Snow leopards eat giant panda cubs if they can catch them.

If the weather is too cold, or the plants get a disease, the **bamboo** dies. When this happens, giant pandas can die because they have no food.

If there is no bamboo, giant pandas have nothing to eat.

Hunting and trapping

In the past, people trapped and killed giant pandas for their fur and meat. Now it is against the law to kill pandas, but some hunters still do.

This policeman has taken a panda skin away from a hunter.

This man has found a trap that is used to catch giant pandas.

Some pandas are hurt by accident. Hunters put down traps to catch other animals, such as deer. Giant pandas get badly injured if they step on the traps.

Dangers to the giant panda's world

Trees in China's mountain forests are being cut down. People are selling the wood and building towns on the land.

Destroying the forests means less food and less space for pandas.

18

Once a year, **male** pandas search for a **female** to **mate** with. If there are towns in the way, pandas cannot find each other easily. Fewer **cubs** are born.

These people are helping a giant panda in a tree.

How many giant pandas are there?

There are about 1,600 giant pandas in the wild today. They all live alone. Most live in small areas with fewer than 20 other pandas living nearby.

Year

1980s

2004

The number of pandas is slowly growing, but there are still not many of them.

 = 500

There are more people in China today than ever before. They use more wood and take more land to live on.

We need to protect the giant pandas' **habitat** to save them.

How are giant pandas being saved?

China has made more than 50 **reserves** for giant pandas. Reserves are areas of land where wild animals such as giant pandas can live in safety.

In reserves, people are not allowed to cut down trees.

Some reserves have **breeding centres** like this one.

In China it is against the law to hunt giant pandas. People called **wardens** protect the giant pandas in their reserve and keep hunters out.

Who is helping giant pandas?

WWF is a **charity**. It is showing people in China how to raise money to protect pandas. Today, tourists pay to watch the pandas.

The giant panda is the symbol of WWF.

Wardens look carefully to find out where giant pandas live.

In the Qinling (you say "Chinling") Mountains, there are 12 new panda **reserves**. The pandas can move safely from one reserve to another.

How can you help?

It is important to know that giant pandas are in danger. Then you can learn how to help to save them. Read, watch, and find out all you can about giant pandas.

It is important to learn how to help save pandas, so that they will not become **extinct**.

26

Here are some things you can do
to help.

- Join a group such as **WWF** that raises
  money for giant panda projects.
- Visit zoos where giant pandas live.
  Some zoos raise money to help wild
  giant pandas.

The future for giant pandas

Giant pandas may soon become **extinct**. In China, about half of all pandas live in **reserves**. More pandas will be saved if their **habitat** is protected.

Giant pandas could become extinct if we do not protect their habitat.

Giant pandas are having **cubs** in safe **breeding centres** in China. Some of these pandas will be set free, into the wild. Then there will be more pandas.

Breeding centres give pandas a safe place to have their babies.

Giant panda facts

- Giant pandas live for about 25 years in the wild.
- A new-born panda **cub** is only as long as a pencil.
- When giant panda cubs are born, they are pink and have no hair.
- Giant pandas are good climbers. They are also good swimmers.

More books to read

Giant Panda, Anna Claybourne (Heinemann, 2005)

Giant Panda, Edana Eckart (Children's Press, 2003)

Panda in the Park, Lucy Daniels (Hodder Children's Books, 2004)

Websites

To find out more about **WWF**, visit their website:
www.wwf.org

Glossary

bamboo a tall plant with green leaves. Pandas eat only bamboo.

breeding centre safe place where male and female animals can mate and have babies

charity group that collects money to help animals or people in need

cub baby panda

extinct when all the animals in a species die out and the species no longer exists

female animal that can become a mother when it grows up. Women and girls are female people.

habitat place where plants and animals grow and live. A forest is a kind of habitat.

mammal animal that feeds its babies with the mother's milk and has some hair on its body

male animal that can become a father when it grows up. Men and boys are male people.

mate what male and female animals do to make babies

reserve area of land where animals are protected and the habitat is looked after

shoot beginning of a new plant

species group of animals that look similar and can have babies together

warden person who guards reserves

WWF charity that used to be called the World Wildlife Fund

Index